When Lambs Turn Into Lions
Discover How The Quiet Lamb Becomes the Ultimate Symbol of Power

CJC PUBLISHING COMPANY

1208 Sumac Dr.
El Paso, TX 79925

Copyright © 2025 by Mikel Brown. All rights reserved
Printed in the United States of America

ISBN: 978-1-930388-29-1

Editorial assistance for CJC Publishing Co.
Cover designed by Charles J. Bennett III for CJC Publishing Co.

All scripture is quoted from the King James Version, New King James Version, New International Version, and the New Living Translation of the Bible.

No part of this publication may be reproduced, stored in a retrieval system, or transmitted in any form or by any means, electronic, mechanical, photocopying, recording, scanning, or otherwise, except as permitted under Section 107 or 108 of the 1976 United States Copyright Act, without the prior written permission of the Published. Requests to the Publisher for permission should be addressed to the Permissions Department, CJC Publishing, 1208 Sumac Drive El Paso, TX 79925, 915-595-137, fax 915-595-1493, or e-mail permcoordinator@cjcpublishing.com.

Limit of Liability/Disclaimer of Warranty: While the publisher and author have used their best efforts in preparing this book, they make no representation or warranties with respect to the accuracy or completeness of the contents of this book and specifically disclaim any implied guarantees. The advice and strategies contained herein may not be suitable for every situation. Neither the publisher nor author shall be liable for any outcome concerning ones finances or business, included but not limited to special, incidental, consequential, or other damages.

FOREWORD BY DR. JOSEPH L. GARLINGTON

WHEN LAMBS
TURN INTO
LIONS

DISCOVER HOW THE QUIET LAMB BECOMES
THE ULTIMATE SYMBOL OF POWER

DR. MIKEL BROWN

EL PASO, TEXAS

AUTOGRAPH

Table of Content

Dedication	*vi*
Foreword	*vii*
Preface	*xi*

CHAPTER 1: The Wow Factor In Balancing Characteristics	13
CHAPTER 2: When Lambs Transform Into Lions	23
CHAPTER 3: Meek Courage But Majestic Strength	31
CHAPTER 4: How The Lion Executes Bold Leadership Moves	39
CHAPTER 5: The Lamb's Dominion Through Gentle Authority	49
CHAPTER 6: Stand Up As A Lion King	57
CHAPTER 7: The Lion's Instinct To Crush Its Enemies	69
CHAPTER 8: The Hybridity Of The Lion And The Lamb	79
CHAPTER 9: Embodying Dual Mastery In Leadership And Life	89
CHAPTER 10: A Study of Silent Authority and Gentle Power	99
CHAPTER 11: Lessons For Life, Business, and Beyond	107
CHAPTER 12: My Personal Transformation From Lamb To Lion	125

Platinum Principles	135
About The Author	137

DEDICATION

I dedicate this book to my incredible and amazing wife and best friend, children, grandchildren, great-grandchildren, and to the entire Joy Nation and ECCM family, who stand with me as lions for the Kingdom of God.

FOREWORD

The ancient Greeks used the word praus to describe a powerful horse they rigorously trained for battle readiness, when it could demonstrate the ability to wait for the command under pressure. However, in the New Testament, that word describes our Lord's character during His earthly ministry. When someone uses meek to explain a weak personality, they are demonstrating a common misunderstanding of using this word and conflating it with one who is simply timid. When one considers the two accounts of the Lord overturning the tables of the merchandisers, who were abusing the Temple, it's difficult to conclude that this Person was weak. The Person who overturned tables in the Temple was not weak, nor was the

Person who hung on the cross while restraining His innate power to stop the whole process. He was the Lamb.

My dear friend, Dr. Mikel Brown, utilizes his various skills and insights as a profound expositor of the Scriptures, his experience as a military noncommissioned officer, and his consistent success as an entrepreneur who has mentored many others with these insights for success in business and life. Dr. Mikel Brown is the founding pastor of Christian Joy Center, a thriving cross-cultural church in the heart of El Paso, Texas, and the leader of a growing network of churches in various parts of the nation. He is a mentor to many eager young people who, through his watchful care and business acumen, have become successful businessmen and businesswomen, many of them in their late teens and early twenties.

When Lambs Turn Into Lions: Discover How The Quiet Lamb Becomes The Ultimate Symbol Of Power is a manual for achieving genuine goals in life and business. He skillfully uses principles clearly articulated in life and the animal kingdom to lead his readers to a profound insight that he has seen in his intriguing study of lions. The Lion and the Lamb are eternal archetypes we see in the Bible and the world around us. I suggest it is the consummate description of the most successful Lion and Lamb entrepreneur in history: The Lord Jesus leveraged principles articulated in this book and produced the most incredible enterprise the world has ever seen: His Church. Dr. Brown's insights will inspire, motivate, and encourage you to unleash your innate lion.

Bishop Joseph L. Garlington
Founder and President of Hosanna House, Inc. and Presiding Bishop of Reconciliation International Network

PREFACE

This book, "When Lambs Turn Into Lions," was written from the depths of my heart for the body of Christ, and every person that will inevitably be conveyed from the kingdom of darkness and into the kingdom of God's dear Son, Jesus. My love for the church that Jesus built is immeasurable, and my desire is to see it rise from its slumber is immense.

We are called to be fierce lions in a world consumed by vicious evil men and women, but we must be ready to stand out as a beacon of divine light in a dark world.

The church will not lose its resilience and strength under the watch of Spirit-filled and committed believers. The church is gifted to be humble but anointed to be lions in business. We must contend for the faith that was once delivered to the saints.

Believers must seek God to be effective in business, commerce, and dominate the economy because true success is rooted in His principles. Jesus exemplified wisdom, integrity, and leadership—qualities that should guide our every decision. The world often steals God's business principles, using concepts like stewardship, diligence, and vision, but leaves God out of the equation.

As believers, we are called to integrate His truth into every area of life, not just within the church. We should actively engage in finance and banking, politics, entertainment, medicine, education, and beyond, bringing God's wisdom and influence into every sector, transforming culture with His Kingdom principles.

CHAPTER 1

THE WOW FACTOR IN BALANCING CHARACTERISTICS

"Learn to command respect like a lion, offer solace like a lamb, but master both for success." — Dr. Mikel Brown

THE WOW FACTOR IN BALANCING CHARACTERISTICS

God and relying on the power of creativity and perseverance stands firm, seeking no shortcuts or escape routes. It doesn't call external crutches a blessing because true internal strength requires no aid beyond the Lord's provision. Every person has a innate ability to rise, but the fierceness to rise must come from the lion within.

You must embrace the Courage and Determination of the lion. So, let's first explore the lion. Known for its bravery and leadership, the lion exemplifies the courage to make bold decisions, the tenacity to overcome obstacles, and the ability to inspire others. A striking example of this courage can be seen in the life of Jesus. Throughout His ministry, He faced opposition and adversity but never wavered in His mission. He boldly confronted injustice and challenged the status quo, embodying the essence of a lion.

Consider the story of a young entrepreneur who encountered numerous setbacks while pitching her innovative tech startup. Each rejection felt like a barrier blocking her path. Yet, like Jesus, she summoned her inner lion, learning from every "no," refining her approach, and discovering new ways to connect with potential investors. Her determination ultimately led to securing funding that propelled her venture to new heights.

In your journey, remember that true courage doesn't mean being free of fear; it means using that fear as fuel for your ambition. Ask yourself in challenging moments: "What would a lion do?" This simple question can shift your mindset and motivate you to take bold action.

Now, the lamb's wisdom, patience and compassion is no joke. As we turn our attention to the lamb, lets pick up on the lamb's subtle approach to life. The lamb teaches us the significance of patience and compassion. In a fast-paced world that often celebrates relentless hustle, it's easy to overlook the value of stepping back and nurturing

THE WOW FACTOR IN BALANCING CHARACTERISTICS

relationships. Jesus exemplified this principle through His ministry, often taking time to connect with individuals, listening to their struggles, and offering support. His compassion for the marginalized and downtrodden resonated deeply, creating a loyal following of believers who admired His kindness.

Consider a small business owner who, in his rush to grow, neglected the importance of fostering connections with his employees. The outcome is a high turnover rate and a toxic atmosphere. After a moment of reflection, he embraced the wisdom of the lamb, investing time in his team, listening to their concerns, and nurturing a supportive culture. This shift not only improved morale but also enhanced productivity and loyalty.

As you pursue your goals, remember that building a multi-million dollar business isn't solely about profits; it's about people. Cultivate patience in your interactions and compassion in your leadership. Recognize that every relationship holds the potential to elevate your business.

BALANCING THE TWO: A HARMONIOUS APPROACH

The true power lies in harmonizing the fierce

determination of the lion with the gentle wisdom of the lamb. Picture a leader who strides confidently into a meeting, prepared to make bold decisions while simultaneously valuing the diverse perspectives of their team. This leader embodies the duality of the roar and the calm, creating an environment where innovation flourishes.

Jesus masterfully balanced these traits throughout His ministry. He demonstrated authority and conviction when teaching profound truths, yet He also exhibited tender care for those in need. One powerful principle to guide you in achieving this balance is the practice of reflective listening. When engaging with others, take time to genuinely understand their viewpoints. This fosters trust and opens doors to creative solutions that may have otherwise gone unnoticed.

CHARACTER PRINCIPLES: YOUR COMPASS

As you navigate this journey of combining the lion's courage with the lamb's wisdom, let character principles be your guiding compass. Integrity, authenticity, and resilience are vital pillars that will steer you through the complexities of life and business.

THE WOW FACTOR IN BALANCING CHARACTERISTICS

For example, integrity involves staying true to your values, even in challenging situations. Authenticity allows you to connect with others more meaningfully, fostering trust and loyalty. Resilience equips you to rebound from setbacks, transforming adversity into opportunity.

Consider the instance of a business leader facing a crisis when a product recall threatened to mar their reputation. Instead of evading the issue, they stood firm in their integrity, communicating transparently with customers and taking prompt action to resolve the situation. Their commitment to authenticity not only salvaged the company's reputation but also forged a stronger bond with their customer base.

We can learn a lot about how these two principle characters go about reducing stress and frustration. The journey to success is often fraught with stress and frustration. However, integrating the principles of the lion and the lamb into your life can help you navigate these challenges with greater ease.

Start by practicing mindfulness, a technique that encourages grounding in the present moment. This can include deep breathing, meditation, or engaging in activities that bring you joy. Mindfulness nurtures resilience, enabling you to respond to stress with clarity rather than reactivity.

Additionally, cultivate a supportive network. Surround yourself with individuals who embody the characteristics of both the lion and the lamb. These relationships will provide encouragement, guidance, and perspective as you navigate your entrepreneurial journey.

As we wrap up this chapter, I encourage you to reflect on the qualities of the lion and the lamb within you. Are you ready to embrace courage while embodying compassion? Are you prepared to lead with integrity and inspire those around you?

The road to building a successful business and leading an effective life is not a straightforward path. It is a journey filled with twists, turns, and invaluable lessons. By harnessing the strengths of both the lion and the lamb, you will not only mitigate stress and frustration but also foster a fulfilling life marked by achievement and meaningful connections.

So, let your journey begin. Let the roar of your ambition echo through the valleys of challenge, and let the gentle strength of your character guide you through the peaks of

THE WOW FACTOR IN BALANCING CHARACTERISTICS

success. The world awaits your unique contribution—embrace it with the heart of a lion and the wisdom of a lamb, just as Jesus did in His ministry. Your multi-million dollar business is merely the beginning.

CHAPTER 2

WHEN LAMBS TRANSFORM INTO LIONS

"The Lamb's grace transforms into the Lion's unstoppable courage." — Dr. Mikel Brown

WHEN LAMBS TRANSFORM INTO LIONS

The Lamb, embodying humility and grace, transforms into the Lion when faced with opposition. His quiet strength ignites, revealing fierce courage, bold authority, and unstoppable power, defending righteousness with unmatched greatness.

Every born-again believer today should reflect the transformative nature of the Lamb and the Lion. With unwavering devotion to God, we embody the humility, grace, and gentleness of the Lamb. Yet, when faced with spiritual battles, we must rise with the boldness, courage, and authority of the Lion.

This dual nature empowers us to conquer the devil and overcome opposition. Through steadfast faith, we fiercely defend righteousness, standing strong in God's power while remaining grounded in love and humility. In this way, we become bold warriors in spirit, committed to advancing God's kingdom with unshakable resolve.

The believer, empowered by the Spirit of God, walks as a force cloaked in meekness yet unrelenting in purpose, destiny, and righteousness. This divine balance is a reflection of Christ's own nature—the Lamb who was sacrificed yet the Lion who reigns. Though clothed in humility, the believer's true strength lies in an unreserved commitment to fulfilling God's will. They are called to embrace the weakest among their community, extending love, grace, and protection to all, especially children, the vulnerable, and those entrusted to their care.

In the defense of children, wealth, and the sanctity of marriage, the believer is both nurturing and fiercely protective. Children represent the future of God's kingdom, marriage the sacred covenant, and wealth the resources entrusted for kingdom advancement. To allow any harm or distortion in these areas is to compromise the values of God's kingdom. Like a lion guarding its pride, the believer stands as an unyielding protector, ready to confront any force that threatens these vital aspects of life.

WHEN LAMBS TRANSFORM INTO LIONS

No weakness is to be shown in this spiritual battle—not even the slightest hint of retreat. With the authority and boldness of a lion, the believer stands firm, enforcing God's word with courage and precision. Their strength lies in their devotion to righteousness, ensuring that God's Word prevails in every circumstance. In the face of challenges, they rise boldly, unafraid, and unashamed, reflecting the majesty of Christ as both Lamb and Lion.

As believers, we are called to live a life of paradoxical strength—what the world perceives as weakness is, in fact, a divine power cloaked in humility. Matthew 5:5 tells us, "Blessed are the meek, for they shall inherit the earth." Meekness is not weakness; it's strength under control. Like a lion who could easily destroy, but chooses to protect. That is the nature of Christ in us—the Lion and the Lamb. We are to be unreserved in our purpose, destiny, and righteousness, fully embracing who God has called us to be.

The Apostle Paul said in 2 Corinthians 12:9, "My grace is sufficient for you, for my power is made perfect in weakness." This isn't a call to shrink back but to rise with the understanding that God's power flows through those willing to be vessels of both grace and strength. Just as Christ fiercely defended children and the vulnerable (Matthew 19:14), so too must we stand guard over our own families, marriages, and resources. These are not mere possessions or relationships—they are God-given responsibilities we are called to defend with the heart of a lion.

I often speak of the necessity of taking on responsibility, facing suffering head-on, and bearing burdens with purpose. As believers, we understand this even more profoundly. Our purpose is eternal, and we carry the weight of representing God's kingdom on earth. To do so effectively, we must combine wisdom, courage, and compassion. Jordan Peterson rightly points out that meaning is found in responsibility, but Scripture elevates this truth—our meaning is found in taking responsibility for the advancement of God's kingdom and the defense of His truth.

Now, let's close this thought with the wit and wisdom of Zig Ziglar: "You were designed for accomplishment, engineered for success, and endowed with the seeds of greatness." God has placed His greatness within you, and you have everything you need to fulfill your destiny. It's time to stand up, stand out, and stand firm. Like a lion standing over its pride, never wavering, never flinching—your strength comes from the Lord, and you are equipped to conquer. The world may see meekness, but heaven knows the lion within. Let your life roar with purpose, defend what matters most, and never forget—God's word will prevail through you.

CHAPTER 3

MEEK COURAGE BUT MAJESTIC STRENGTH

"Humility roots you; boldness empowers you to reign as a lion." — *Dr. Mikel Brown*

MEEK COURAGE BUT MAJESTIC STRENGTH

The balance between these two characteristics of both the lion and the lamb is essential for thriving in life, business, and spiritual warfare. While we are called to be humble as children of God, there are moments when humility must give way to righteous strength. In the context of life and business, humility should never be mistaken for passivity or weakness. Understanding the dual nature of the Lamb and the Lion can empower believers to act with wisdom, boldness, and authority, while remaining rooted in the grace of Christ.

HUMILITY OF THE LAMB: A FOUNDATION IN GOD

Jesus, the Lamb of God, is the ultimate example of

humility. As Philippians 2:6-8 teaches, Jesus "did not consider equality with God something to be grasped but made Himself nothing, taking the very nature of a servant." This is the model for how we should relate to others, especially within the body of Christ. C.S. Lewis once said, "Humility is not thinking less of ourselves, but thinking of ourselves less." It is serving others, lifting them up, and displaying kindness and gentleness, just as a lamb moves without malice or aggression.

In life, believers are called to be lambs with other lambs—expressing grace, forgiveness, and love to one another. This is especially crucial within the church and the Christian community, where relationships are nurtured through mutual humility. We are to be gentle in speech, patient in spirit, and quick to forgive, as Paul exhorts in Ephesians 4:2, "Be completely humble and gentle; be patient, bearing with one another in love."

However, this same lamb-like humility must not be mistaken for weakness in other spheres, particularly in life and business. In these arenas, the nature of the Lion must rise within the believer. The lion is not only a symbol of strength but also wisdom, courage, and the ability to discern when to act decisively.

MEEK COURAGE BUT MAJESTIC STRENGTH

THE BOLDNESS OF THE LION: RULING WITH STRENGTH AND WISDOM

In the marketplace, humility is essential, but believers cannot afford to be overly humble to the point where they fail to stand up for what is right, make bold decisions, or protect their interests. The lion, often seen as the king of the jungle, is not merely aggressive for the sake of aggression, but its boldness is tempered with precision, purpose, and discernment.

In business, Christians must adopt the mindset of the lion. This means being assertive, taking charge of situations, and confidently pursuing goals. Proverbs 28:1 declares, "The righteous are as bold as a lion." This boldness is not arrogance, but a confidence that comes from knowing who we are in Christ and that He has given us the authority to succeed and to lead.

The lion doesn't retreat when faced with a challenge; instead, it stands firm, assesses the situation, and strikes with power when necessary. In the same way, Christian leaders in business must be prepared to make tough decisions and defend their values, even when opposed by others. The lion in the believer is also a protector—guarding their business, their family, and their integrity against all attacks.

However, the lion's strength should never diminish the humility of the lamb. The true power of the lion is not in constant aggression but in the ability to defend and reconcile when needed.

THE LION AND THE LAMB IN SPIRITUAL WARFARE

The Christian life is a battlefield, and believers must understand that we cannot afford to be uninformed, misinformed, or unfamiliar with the weapons of our warfare. As Paul writes in Ephesians 6:12, "For we do not wrestle against flesh and blood, but against the rulers, against the authorities, against the cosmic powers over this present darkness."

While humility keeps us grounded and reliant on God, the boldness of the lion equips us to stand firm in spiritual warfare. We are not called to be passive victims of the enemy's attacks but to confront him head-on. This is where the dual nature of the lamb and the lion is critical. The lamb in us seeks peace and reconciliation, but when the enemy—the opposing lamb—reveals its horns, we must

MEEK COURAGE BUT MAJESTIC STRENGTH

transform into the lion, ready to defend our faith, our families, and our destiny with aggression and precision.

Christians must be well-versed in the weapons of spiritual warfare: prayer, fasting, the Word of God, and the power of the Holy Spirit. These are our tools for victory. We cannot afford to be ignorant of the devil's schemes, as 2 Corinthians 2:11 warns us. We must be vigilant, always ready to defend, but also to reconcile.

RECONCILING WITH THE STRENGTH OF A LION

While the lion in us is called to defend against attack, it is also called to reconcile. A true believer does not seek conflict for the sake of conflict but understands that peace, when possible, is always the best resolution. As Romans 12:18 says, "If it is possible, as far as it depends on you, live at peace with everyone."

When a fellow believer or even a business partner reveals their horns, the lion must rise to defend what is right, but also seek to reconcile, bringing restoration where possible. This is the brilliance of the lion's leadership—it knows when to strike, but it also knows when to gather and nurture its pride.

WHEN LAMBS TURN INTO LIONS

BOLD AS LIONS, GENTLE AS LAMBS

The Christian life is a delicate balance between the humility of the lamb and the boldness of the lion. In business, life, and spiritual warfare, we are called to be lambs with lambs, extending grace, love, and forgiveness. But when opposition arises, and the devil shows his horns, we must rise as lions, ready to defend our values, protect the vulnerable, and stand firm in our purpose.

A believer cannot afford to be uninformed or passive. Like the lion, we must be strategic, courageous, and fierce when necessary, yet always with a heart that seeks reconciliation, just as Christ did. In every aspect of life, business, and faith, we are called to embody both the Lamb and the Lion—gentle in spirit, yet powerful in purpose.

CHAPTER 4

HOW THE LION EXECUTES BOLD LEADERSHIP MOVES

"Humility grounds us; boldness leads us in life's fiercest battles." — Dr. Mikel Brown

HOW THE LION EXECUTES BOLD LEADERSHIP MOVES

A believer, like the lion, must be bold, decisive, and intentional in every aspect of life. The lion is not just the king of the jungle because of its size or power, but because of its mastery in executing leadership. The lion rules with wisdom, strategy, and purpose, balancing strength with protection, and aggression with nurturing. In the same way, a believer should learn from the lion's leadership, applying these qualities to life, business, and spiritual growth. The characteristics of a lion in the wild reflect the qualities a believer must harness to live a life of significance, purpose, and influence.

THE LION'S BOLDNESS: FEARLESS LEADERSHIP

WHEN LAMBS TURN INTO LIONS

The lion embodies boldness, a necessary trait for leadership. Proverbs 28:1 says, "The wicked flee when no one pursues, but the righteous are bold as a lion." This scripture underscores the connection between righteousness and boldness. A believer's boldness doesn't come from self-confidence, but from a deep-rooted understanding of who they are in Christ. When you know your identity in God, fear cannot paralyze you, and you can step out in bold faith, just as the lion steps into battle without fear.

In life, a believer is called to take bold moves. Whether it's making tough decisions, standing up for what is right, or taking risks in business, a true believer must have the courage to act when others hesitate. Bold leadership means knowing the direction you're heading in and confidently leading others, even in the face of adversity. The lion doesn't second-guess its decisions, and neither should you. As believers, we are called to lead with authority, fully trusting in the guidance of the Holy Spirit.

STRATEGIC MOVES: GOVERNING WITH PRECISION

Lions govern their pride with strategy, much like a wise

HOW THE LION EXECUTES BOLD LEADERSHIP MOVES

leader governs their community or business. They are not haphazard or reckless but understand the importance of precision and timing. Lions execute their attacks with skill and patience. They observe, calculate, and then strike at the opportune moment. Similarly, a believer must govern their life and decisions with strategy. Proverbs 16:9 tells us, "The heart of man plans his way, but the Lord establishes his steps." This means that while we must make plans and be strategic, our steps must be rooted in God's wisdom.

Leadership in life means being strategic in the way we handle resources, time, relationships, and opportunities. Just as a lion surveys the environment before making a move, a believer must seek God's wisdom and discernment in all they do. Reckless decisions lead to chaos, but strategic leadership—guided by the Holy Spirit—leads to prosperity and success. Bold leadership is not about constant action; it's about knowing when to move and when to wait, when to push and when to pull back. Like the lion, believers must be wise, deliberate, and decisive in all areas of life.

STRENGTH IN COMMUNITY: BUILDING AND

WHEN LAMBS TURN INTO LIONS

PROTECTING THE PRIDE

Lions are not solitary animals; they thrive in the context of community. They understand that the strength of the pride is in unity. The lion takes responsibility not only for itself but for its pride, ensuring that the younger lions are nurtured and protected while maintaining the pride's stability. This aspect of the lion's nature teaches believers about the importance of community and mentorship.

In life and leadership, a believer must take responsibility for their community—their family, church, business, or organization. Strong leaders don't lead for themselves but for the benefit of those they are entrusted with. Just as the lion ensures that the next generation of lions grows strong and capable, a believer must invest in and mentor others. Effective leadership is about raising others up, empowering them to reach their potential, and providing the protection they need to flourish.

The lion protects its pride from external threats, and in the same way, a believer must be vigilant in protecting their community from negative influences or spiritual attacks. Bold leadership is not just about personal success but ensuring the growth and safety of those around you. As Christ protects His church, so too should believers protect their families, businesses, and communities with the ferocity of a lion.

BOLD LEADERSHIP IN THE WILD: FACING CHALLENGES WITH DETERMINATION

In the wild, lions face constant threats—from rival predators to the harshness of nature. Yet, they remain unshaken. They face these challenges with determination, adapting and surviving because they are built for it. Likewise, believers must recognize that challenges in life are inevitable. Adversity, failure, and opposition will come, but like the lion, we are built to overcome them. James 1:12 says, "Blessed is the one who perseveres under trial because, having stood the test, that person will receive the crown of life."

Bold leadership means understanding that difficulties are part of the journey, but they are not a reason to retreat. The lion knows it must fight to maintain its territory and survive, and as believers, we must fight to maintain our spiritual, personal, and professional territories. We fight with prayer, perseverance, and a steadfast belief that God has already equipped us to overcome every obstacle. The lion doesn't back down from a challenge, and neither should we.

AGGRESSIVE IN DEFENDING BUT COMPASSIONATE IN RECONCILIATION

While the lion is aggressive in defending its pride, it also knows how to balance this strength with compassion. Within its pride, there is order, care, and a deep sense of responsibility for each member. A true leader understands that there is a time to be aggressive and a time to be compassionate. Jesus, who is both the Lion of Judah and the Lamb of God, showed this balance perfectly. In one moment, He turned over tables in the temple, and in another, He gently restored the woman caught in adultery.

Believers must understand that bold leadership does not mean being harsh or overbearing. There is a time for confrontation, but there is also a time for reconciliation. When a fellow believer stumbles, we are called not only to correct but to restore. Like the lion, we protect what is ours with strength, but we nurture and build up those within our pride with love and compassion.

LEADING WITH AUTHORITY: THE LION'S EXAMPLE IN BUSINESS AND LIFE

In business, bold leadership looks like taking charge of situations, making tough decisions, and pushing forward in faith when others are paralyzed by fear. A believer must not be afraid to lead with authority. God has given us the mandate to be leaders in every area of our lives. We are called to be the head and not the tail, above and not beneath (Deuteronomy 28:13).

The lion leads its pride with the confidence that it is in control, and as believers, we must step into every situation with the same confidence that God has given us authority. When you walk into a room, understand that you carry the authority of the Lion of Judah within you. You are not there by accident, and God has equipped you to lead with power and influence.

THE LION'S BOLD LEADERSHIP

Bold leadership, like the lion's, is about balance. It's about

WHEN LAMBS TURN INTO LIONS

knowing when to be aggressive and when to be compassionate, when to act and when to wait. It's about leading not just for your benefit but for the growth and protection of those around you. Believers are called to be lions—bold, strategic, and fearless leaders in every area of life. You are equipped with the strength, wisdom, and authority of Christ Himself. Rise up, lead boldly, and rule with the confidence that comes from knowing who you are and whose you are. The world is waiting for your roar.

CHAPTER 5

THE LAMB'S DOMINION THROUGH GENTLE AUTHORITY

"In unity, lambs rise as an impenetrable force of purpose." — Dr. Mikel Brown

THE LAMB'S DOMINION THROUGH GENTLE AUTHORITY

The lamb, often perceived as gentle and meek, is a powerful symbol in the life of a believer. It embodies the qualities of humility, patience, and peace. Yet, in its unassuming nature lies a hidden strength that far surpasses what meets the eye.

The lamb's power is not found in outward aggression, but in its quiet resilience and unwavering resolve. It is a power that reveals itself at the right moment, often surprising those who misjudge it. Christians are called to emulate this same covert strength—meek on the surface, but prepared to rise with quiet authority when necessary.

At first glance, a lamb may appear fragile and defenseless.

WHEN LAMBS TURN INTO LIONS

However, the true strength of the lamb is in its unity. Alone, a lamb may seem vulnerable, but when united with others, they form an impenetrable force. Their unity is their shield, their collective wisdom their guide. Just as believers are called to be "wise as serpents and harmless as doves" (Matthew 10:16), the lamb teaches us that wisdom lies not in outward displays of power, but in subtle, strategic movements. The strength of the lamb is revealed in moments of assumed weakness, when the world least expects it.

Imagine walking through life as a believer, where many perceive your humility as weakness. They may mistake your kindness for passivity, your quietness for ignorance. But here's the key—your power is hidden, intentionally reserved, waiting for the right moment to emerge. You don't need to prove your strength at every turn because you know the strength that resides within you is not defined by outward aggression but by your unwavering connection to God's purpose.

When challenges come and others assume you are too weak to handle them, that's when the power of the lamb

THE LAMB'S DOMINION THROUGH GENTLE AUTHORITY

reveals itself. You see, the lamb doesn't fight in the way the world expects it to. It doesn't rely on brute force or loud declarations. Instead, it moves with wisdom, acting when the time is right, and confounding those who underestimated it. This is the kind of strength believers are called to wield—the strength that remains calm in the storm, confident that God is at work behind the scenes.

In the same way, as Christians, we are often underestimated in the world. The world may see our humility as weakness, but that's where they are wrong. Our humility is not a sign of weakness, it is the cover for a much deeper, much more profound strength. It's the power of knowing who we are in Christ, a power that is not swayed by the opinions or expectations of others. We are lambs in the hands of a mighty Shepherd, guided by divine wisdom that gives us the advantage in every situation.

When you walk into a room and others assume you don't have the strength to lead or the insight to succeed, that's when your hidden power shines. You don't need to boast or demand attention, because your authority comes from a deeper source. Like the lamb, your strength is quiet but resolute, waiting for the right moment to reveal itself. And when the time comes, when ignorance and weakness are assumed, that's when you rise. Not with arrogance, but with a calm and steady force that shakes the very foundations of doubt.

It's the same power Jesus exemplified—He was the Lamb of God, humble, unassuming, and yet filled with divine authority. His strength wasn't in the loudness of His voice but in the purpose of His mission. He didn't need to prove Himself because His identity was rooted in something far greater than earthly recognition. And when it was time, He laid down His life, showing that true power is not in the ability to dominate, but in the ability to surrender with purpose.

That's the kind of power believers are called to wield. A strength that's not loud, but profound. A strength that's not boastful, but impactful. When the world thinks you're weak, that's when your power is revealed—not in aggression, but in wisdom, patience, and strategic action. The lamb's power is its ability to surprise, to rise when least expected, and to overcome not with force, but with purpose.

THE LAMB'S DOMINION THROUGH GENTLE AUTHORITY

You don't need to roar to prove your strength. The power of the lamb is in its quiet resilience, its unity, and its deep-rooted connection to something greater than itself. That's the power of a believer. You may be underestimated, but never overlook the hidden strength within. Your power lies in your purpose, and when it's time, the world will see the quiet strength of the lamb rise, not as a victim but as a victor.

: CHAPTER 6

STAND UP AS A LION KING

"Through challenges, resilience is built; through faith, the lion emerges." —Dr. Mikel Brown

STAND UP AS A LION KING

The rise and development of a lion from a cub to a full-grown, majestic king of the jungle is one of nature's most powerful and awe-inspiring journeys. It is a life shaped by trials, resilience, and purpose, mirroring the profound story of Christ and the transformative path of the believer. From the innocence of a young cub to the powerful presence of a fully grown lion, this growth process reflects the Christian's spiritual journey a journey that reveals who we truly are beneath the surface and calls us to embrace our identity as both kings and warriors in this world.

The Early Days of a lion is one of Innocence and

WHEN LAMBS TURN INTO LIONS

Dependence. A lion cub is born into the world weak, vulnerable, and entirely dependent on its mother and the pride for survival. During these early stages, the cub's primary focus is learning the basics of life—how to hunt, how to interact with others, and how to avoid danger. The cub doesn't know it yet, but within its small frame lies the potential for greatness. The same is true for every believer in Christ. In the early stages of our spiritual journey, we may feel vulnerable and unaware of the magnitude of the power that lies within us. We are dependent on our heavenly Father, just as the cub depends on its pride.

But here's the beautiful truth: even in our weakness, even in our dependence, God is already shaping us into who we are meant to be. The cub may not yet have the physical strength of a lion, but its destiny is already written in its DNA. It is meant to rise, to grow, and to reign. And so are we. As Christians, our true identity is not determined by our current weakness or struggles, but by our spiritual DNA—we are children of God, heirs to His kingdom, and destined to reign alongside Christ, the Lion of Judah (Revelation 5:5).

All lions will inevitably experience a Season of Training to develop Strength and Discipline. All you have to do is watch the Lion King Movie to see this reality. Laugh Out Loud!

As the cub grows, it enters a critical season of training. This is when it begins to develop the skills that will define its future as a lion. Hunting, fighting, and navigating the wild are not instinctive; they are learned through discipline and practice. The cub faces challenges, some that push it to its limits. There are times when it fails, but every failure is a lesson that strengthens its resolve. Slowly but surely, the cub's claws sharpen, its muscles grow stronger, and its instincts become sharper.

Considering, in the same way, believers go through seasons of spiritual training. The Bible speaks of the importance of discipline and perseverance in the life of a Christian. Hebrews 12:11 reminds us that "No discipline seems pleasant at the time, but painful. Later on, however, it produces a harvest of righteousness and peace for those who have been trained by it." Like the lion cub, we must embrace the challenges and hardships of life, knowing that each one is preparing us for the future God has designed for us. The trials we face are not meant to destroy us, but to shape us into the powerful individuals God created us to be.

This period of training is where resilience is built. Resilience is not just the ability to endure; it's the determination to rise again after every fall. Just as the lion cub learns from each failed hunt, each encounter with danger, and each struggle for dominance, so too must Christians learn from their experiences. Failure is not final—it is fuel for growth.

THE COMING OF AGE: STEPPING INTO POWER

As the cub reaches maturity, it begins to step into its power. No longer a follower, the lion becomes a leader, commanding respect through its presence and actions. Its roar, once a playful sound, now echoes across the savannah, announcing its arrival. The lion does not question its identity—it knows it is a king. It carries itself with authority, knowing that it has earned its place at the top of the food chain.

For the believer, reaching spiritual maturity is akin to

stepping into the fullness of our identity in Christ. Ephesians 4:13 speaks of growing "to the measure of the stature of the fullness of Christ." When we fully grasp who we are in Him, we no longer question our authority.

We understand that we are co-heirs with Christ, seated in heavenly places, and empowered to live with boldness and purpose. Just as the lion's roar is a declaration of its presence and power, our lives should be a declaration of God's presence and power within us. When we speak, when we act, it should be with the authority of the King of Kings.

THE LION'S REVOLUTIONARY STRATEGY IS BOLD AND CALCULATED MOVES

One of the most remarkable aspects of a lion's life is its strategy. The lion doesn't waste energy on unnecessary battles or fruitless pursuits. Instead, it observes, calculates, and strikes with precision. Its strength is not in constant activity but in strategic action. When the lion moves, it moves with purpose—whether it's hunting prey or defending its pride, every action is intentional.

For the believer, this is a powerful lesson. Life is not about being busy; it's about being effective. We are called to live with purpose, making strategic moves in our personal lives, our spiritual walks, and our businesses. In Proverbs 3:6 "In all your ways acknowledge Him (God), And He shall direct your paths." Just as the lion waits for the perfect moment to strike, we too must wait for God's timing in our endeavors. But when that moment comes, we must act boldly, without hesitation. This is what it means to live with the heart of a lion—to seize opportunities, to confront challenges head-on, and to move forward with confidence in who we are.

UNVEILING THE TRUE KING BENEATH THE FLESH

For every believer, there is a lion beneath the thin veneer of flesh. The world may see us as ordinary, but beneath the surface, we are kings. We carry within us the spirit of Christ, the Lion of Judah. The flesh may try to hide this reality, making us doubt our strength, our purpose, or our worth. But when we begin to walk in the fullness of our identity, when we allow the lion within us to rise, we become unstoppable.

Jesus Himself exemplified this in His earthly life. On the surface, He appeared as a humble man, unassuming and often underestimated. But beneath that humble exterior was the power of the King of Kings. When it was time to confront sin, death, and the grave, He rose as the Lion of Judah, crushing the head of the enemy with a single, decisive act of victory on the cross. In the same way, as believers, we must understand that beneath our humility lies a powerful identity—one that is destined to reign.

THE LION'S LEGACY: LIVING WITH PURPOSE AND DOMINION

Finally, the fully grown lion lives with a sense of purpose and dominion. It understands that its role is not just to survive but to thrive, to protect its pride, and to rule its territory. In the same way, believers are called to live with purpose and dominion in every area of life. We are not meant to merely exist; we are meant to make an impact. We are called to protect and nurture those around us, to lead with wisdom, and to bring God's kingdom into every sphere we touch.

WHEN LAMBS TURN INTO LIONS

The lion's journey from cub to king is a reflection of the Christian's journey from new believer to spiritual warrior. It is a journey of resilience, training, and ultimately stepping into power and purpose. As we embrace our true identity in Christ, we, like the lion, can rise to crush every obstacle, conquer every challenge, and live as the kings we were created to be. The world may see us as ordinary, but we know the truth—we are lions.

There is a purpose of the lion's ability to roar, and its reason may cause a mental brain freeze but I assure, after hearing my reason and purpose, you'll want to roar as well. A lion doesn't roar because it can—it roars to declare its territory, to send a message that demands attention and commands respect. "A lion has roared! Who will not fear? The Lord God has spoken! Who can but prophesy?" (Amos 3:8 NKJV).

The roar of a lion is not wasted energy; it is precise, powerful, and purposeful. Similarly, a believer must know when to roar—when to speak with the authority of God's Word, not just because they can, but because it's time to establish dominion and declare victory.

STAND UP AS A LION KING

When the believer roars in prophecy, they're not just making noise—they're shifting atmospheres, breaking chains, and declaring God's will with power. It's the roar of destiny, the voice of heaven, unleashing transformation through the Spirit's demonstration. Therefore, Roar with intention. Roar with purpose. Roar with power.

But the roar of the believer isn't merely about volume; it's about the authority behind it. When you speak God's Word, it carries the weight of heaven, shaking foundations and aligning circumstances with God's divine will.

A prophetic roar silences the enemy, making space for God's promises to manifest. It's not the sound, but the substance that counts. A roar backed by faith pierces darkness, propels forward, and brings life. Roar not for attention—roar for transformation and divine breakthrough.

If you are declaring God's divine providence over your life, the life and dominance of your children, over your marriage, over your business and finances; don't roar like a feeble war torn, battle fatigued lion. Roar like the lion after doing all the stand, it stands, making His presence known and heard. ROAR!!!

CHAPTER 7

THE LION'S INSTINCT TO CRUSH ITS ENEMIES

"Bold leadership requires precise action, strategic wisdom, and fearless faith." — Dr. Mikel Brown

THE LION'S INSTINCT TO CRUSH ITS ENEMIES

Imagine a lion in the wild fierce, unyielding, with laser-focused intensity. It surveys its territory, aware of every movement, every sound, every potential threat or opportunity. A lion doesn't just survive; it dominates. It moves with power, precision, and an unstoppable drive. It's not just instinct; it's deliberate action. The lion crushes anything that dares to challenge its authority, protecting its pride and territory with unwavering aggression. This is the mindset every believer must have, not only in their spiritual life but also in business.

In life, the Christian is called to take on the mindset of a lion when it comes to spiritual warfare. The lion is not passive; it doesn't retreat when opposition arises. It stands firm and roars with authority, sending a clear message to its enemies: I will not be moved. As believers, we must embody this ferocity in our spiritual lives.

We cannot afford to be passive when the enemy tries to disrupt our peace, sabotage our faith, or undermine our purpose. The Bible declares in 1 Peter 5:8, "Your adversary the devil prowls around like a roaring lion, seeking someone to devour." But here's the truth—we are the true lions, clothed in the authority of Christ. The enemy may roar, but he cannot stand against a believer who knows their authority. Crush the head of your spiritual enemies with relentless prayer, faith, and the Word of God.

In business, the lion's strategy is equally as vital. The marketplace can be a battleground, full of competitors, challenges, and setbacks. But as a believer in business, you must adopt the mindset of a lion. Bold, fierce, and determined to succeed. When obstacles appear, you don't shrink back—you attack with strategy, resilience, and ferocity.

A lion doesn't apologize for being at the top of the food

THE LION'S INSTINCT TO CRUSH ITS ENEMIES

chain, and neither should you apologize for your ambition and your desire to see your business thrive. You were created to lead, to innovate, and to conquer the obstacles that stand between you and your dreams.

Think about how the lion hunts. It doesn't waste energy on every potential target. Instead, it waits for the perfect moment, carefully calculating its approach. When the time is right, it leaps into action with explosive power, focusing entirely on the prize. This is how you must approach business. Don't be scattered, chasing every opportunity without strategy. Be laser-focused. Identify your target, strategize, and strike with precision.

Whether it's closing a deal, launching a new venture, or expanding your influence, move with the authority of a lion. No half-measures. No hesitation. You see, in business, there will always be competition—people or companies trying to pull you down, distract you, or overtake your success. But you were born to be the lion, born to roar louder, act bolder, and move faster than any opposition.

Here's a powerful truth: The lion is never in a hurry, but it always gets the job done. It moves with purpose, not desperation. And that's how you must move in life and business. No need to rush, but no room for laziness. Each step, each decision, is calculated to bring you closer to your goal. When challenges arise, you don't crumble—you rise to meet them. You see, the lion thrives in the wild, just as you will thrive in the chaos of life's ups and downs. You are not a victim of your circumstances; you are the king of your territory.

And let's be clear—the lion doesn't tolerate anything that threatens its pride or its reign. Likewise, in business, you must not tolerate distractions, mediocrity, or anyone who undermines your vision. If something or someone is hindering your progress, be prepared to eliminate that obstacle swiftly and decisively.

A lion cannot afford to let its enemies linger, and neither can you afford to let anything slow down your momentum. This isn't about aggression for the sake of aggression—this is about survival and dominance. It's about protecting your vision, your dreams, and your business with the same fierceness that a lion protects its territory.

In the spiritual realm, the lion's ferocity is your weapon

THE LION'S INSTINCT TO CRUSH ITS ENEMIES

against the enemy. The devil tries to intimidate and undermine your faith, but like the lion, you rise up and crush his schemes under the weight of your prayers and your faith. Ephesians 6:11 says, "Put on the full armor of God so that you can take your stand against the devil's schemes." This armor transforms you into the lion of the spiritual battlefield, equipped to demolish strongholds, break chains, and roar in victory. You don't fight for victory; you fight from victory because you know the One who has already conquered the grave.

And in business, this same victory mindset applies. The lion doesn't hope for a win—it expects it. It knows its place at the top and fights to maintain it. You must have that same expectation. You're not hoping your business will succeed—you're expecting it to thrive.

Every move you make should be aligned with the belief that your victory is inevitable because you've been given the authority to dominate in your field. Whether you're an entrepreneur, a leader, or a visionary, you are not here to play small—you're here to crush mediocrity, break barriers, and establish yourself as a leader.

WHEN LAMBS TURN INTO LIONS

Let's be real—a lion does not negotiate with its enemies, and you cannot negotiate with failure or mediocrity. You crush it underfoot, like the lion crushes the skull of its prey. If your dream is worth fighting for, then fight like a lion. If your business is worth building, then build like a lion—strong, bold, and unstoppable. Don't retreat. Don't apologize. Move forward with fierce determination, knowing that nothing can stop you except you.

And here's the clincher: A lion's roar can be heard miles away, sending a message of dominance and strength. Your impact, your influence, and your success should be felt far beyond your immediate reach. When you make moves in business or life, make sure they're bold enough to send ripples through your industry, your community, and beyond. Roar with confidence. Roar with authority.

At the end of the day, the lion is a symbol of victory, power, and relentless pursuit. And as a believer, you embody that same spirit. Whether in life, in business, or in your spiritual walk, you are called to crush obstacles, overcome adversities, and roar with confidence and authority. The world is your territory—step into it with the mindset of a

THE LION'S INSTINCT TO CRUSH ITS ENEMIES

lion, knowing that nothing can stand in your way. It is not who will allow you to succeed; it's who is going to stop you from succeeding! Now, go forth, and roar.

CHAPTER 8

THE HYBRIDITY OF THE LION AND THE LAMB

"It is this fluidity, this seamless transition from lion to lamb and back, that transforms people and communities."
— *Dr. Mikel Brown*

THE HYBRIDITY OF THE LION AND THE LAMB

We all have heard, unless your head has been in the sand all your life, that the lion is often regarded as the king of the jungle, a symbol of strength, courage, and leadership. But beneath this powerful exterior lies a profound understanding of the power of one: the idea that both individual and collective actions can lead to transformation, growth, and freedom. The lion's innate wisdom offers a valuable lesson in how to combine intentional thoughts and actions to produce massive changes in one's life, one's environment, and in the corporate and personal realms.

THE POWER OF ONE: HOW THE LION SEES IT

The lion exemplifies the power of one, understanding

that leadership and impact don't always come from vast numbers but often from a single, intentional action. One lion can control the fate of a pride, leading and protecting its members, not just through brute strength, but through calculated decisions and actions. This "power of one" is reflected in how the lion navigates its surroundings with authority and purpose, influencing everything around it.

In a similar way, the power of one can influence our lives. A single, intentional decision can set the stage for transformative outcomes. Just as the lion's roar can command the jungle, a focused thought can change the course of our lives. This is especially important when we consider the merging of thoughts and actions—one must be intentional in aligning thoughts with purposeful, directed action.

The lion understands that just as a single decision can make a difference, so too can small, repeated actions. The lion's daily habits—protecting the pride, hunting with precision, and maintaining its territory—illustrate how consistent actions build lasting success. For us, the key is in identifying those small but powerful actions that, over time,

THE HYBRIDITY OF THE LION AND THE LAMB

bring about monumental change. Whether it's committing to a daily discipline or shifting a mindset to align with success principles, it's these small, intentional choices that lead to massive life transformation.

COMBINING INTENTIONAL THOUGHTS AND ACTIONS

The lion doesn't act without thought. Its strength comes from a deep instinctual wisdom, and we can liken this to how we must combine intentional thinking with strategic action to create real change. There's a phrase often used in leadership: "Think like a lion, act like a lion." This phrase sums up the idea that leadership begins in the mind. Before the lion goes on the hunt, it strategizes—measuring the distance, analyzing the herd, and preparing itself mentally. Similarly, we must align our thoughts to our goals and dreams before we can see them materialize.

Intentional thinking involves visualizing what we want to achieve, framing our mindset for success, and using our thoughts as a blueprint for action. This is not passive daydreaming, but a disciplined mental practice, just as the

WHEN LAMBS TURN INTO LIONS

lion's pre-hunt posture is not lazy lounging but focused readiness. When our thoughts are focused on our desired outcomes, they serve as the foundation for inspired action. The lion's every movement is purposeful; so too must ours be.

Once thoughts are intentionally aligned with purpose, actions must follow. When the lion pounces, it does so with full commitment—no hesitation, no second-guessing. This is how we must approach life when aiming to produce massive change. Fear or doubt can paralyze us from acting, but the lion doesn't hesitate because it knows that success comes through decisive, intentional action. The lesson for us is to commit fully to each step, understanding that our actions have the power to create ripple effects in our environment and our personal lives.

FROM LION TO LAMB AND LAMB TO LION: NOT SEPARATE BUT ONE

The lion also embodies a paradox: the ability to transition from ferocity to gentleness, from the role of king to that of servant. This reflects the dual nature of leadership—sometimes, strength is found in humility and gentleness, and sometimes,

THE HYBRIDITY OF THE LION AND THE LAMB

gentleness must give way to bold action. The lion and the lamb are not separate; they are expressions of the same core power that understands when to wield strength and when to embrace softness.

In the Bible, Jesus is referred to as both the Lion of Judah and the Lamb of God, symbolizing this dual aspect of leadership. As leaders in business, ministry, and life, we must learn to navigate this dynamic. There are times when a leader must be as fierce as a lion, driving forward with purpose, defending their vision, and guiding people with authority. Other times, the leader must be as gentle as a lamb, nurturing their people, leading with compassion, and serving rather than dominating. The ability to transition between these modes is key to building successful kingdom enterprises and leading people to freedom and success.

The lion understands that these two expressions are not mutually exclusive but are instead aspects of the same power. Knowing when to be a lion—strong, commanding, and decisive—and when to be a lamb—humble, serving, and compassionate—is the secret to balanced and effective leadership. In ministry, this dynamic is crucial when leading people (sheep) to freedom and success. Shepherding them requires the wisdom to know when to protect with strength and when to guide with gentleness. It is this fluidity, this seamless transition from lion to lamb and back, that transforms people and communities.

KINGDOM ENTERPRISES: LEADERSHIP THAT TRANSFORMS

Building kingdom enterprises—whether in business, ministry, or any other realm—requires both lion-like strength and lamb-like servanthood. The lion's ability to harness the power of one—both in individual actions and corporate influence—provides a model for kingdom leadership that is bold yet compassionate, decisive yet humble.

A lion leads its pride with authority, but it also knows the importance of unity and teamwork. It doesn't operate in isolation but ensures that every member of the pride plays a role. Similarly, kingdom enterprises thrive when leaders build teams that work together with a shared vision. The lion's understanding of corporate strength teaches us that no matter how powerful an individual leader may be, success comes when everyone is empowered to fulfill their role.

THE HYBRIDITY OF THE LION AND THE LAMB

When building a kingdom enterprise, it's essential to create an environment where people are not just followers but are empowered to lead in their own right. This is how we lead people (the sheep) to freedom and success—by helping them realize their own potential to influence and lead. The lion's leadership is not just about commanding; it's about creating an atmosphere where others can thrive.

CREATING A WEALTH MINDSET: SMALL ACTIONS, BIG IMPACT

The lion's strategic approach teaches us that it's often the small, seemingly insignificant actions that lead to the most significant changes. In life and business, the principle of the "power of one" can be applied to our mindset toward wealth. Wealth, in a kingdom context, isn't just about money; it's about abundance in every area of life—spiritually, mentally, emotionally, and materially. And it begins with the small things.

Just as a lion builds its strength through daily habits and actions, we can cultivate a wealth mindset by making small but intentional choices. These might include daily gratitude, investing time in personal growth, or creating systems that support long-term financial and personal success. The lion knows that every step in the right direction brings it closer to its goal, and we must adopt the same mindset.

A wealth mindset is not about quick, flashy wins; it's about consistent, intentional progress. Whether it's starting a new business, growing spiritually, or leading a community, the lion's wisdom reminds us that greatness comes from a series of well-chosen, disciplined actions over time. The little things—the daily decisions, the intentional focus, the strategic thinking—are what create lasting success and impact.

In conclusion, the lion's understanding of the power of one, the balance between strength and gentleness, and the significance of small, intentional actions offers a profound lesson in leadership and transformation. Whether in business, ministry, or personal life, we can learn from the lion's approach to achieve massive, kingdom-driven change in our lives and the world around us.

CHAPTER 9

EMBODYING DUAL MASTERY IN LEADERSHIP AND LIFE

"In every heart resides a lion's courage," and when summoned, this courage does not just confront, it transforms."
— Dr. Mikel Brown

EMBODYING DUAL MASTERY IN LEADERSHIP AND LIFE

In the complex tapestry of leadership, the imagery of the lion and the lamb offers profound insights into the art of influence and the dynamics of power. These two creatures, seemingly at odds in nature, encapsulate the essence of an ideal leader—powerful yet gentle, commanding yet serene. This duality not only shaped the leadership style of one of history's most pivotal figures, Jesus Christ, but also serves as a pivotal model for modern leadership, especially in the high-stakes environment of business boardrooms.

The lion, majestic and unyielding, does not quiver before ostensible strength. Even against those who boast a mightier roar, the lion stands resolute, its confidence undimmed. It is a creature that challenges not just for dominance but as a guardian of the meek. In its presence, the facade of strength crumbles, revealing the truth that real power lies not in muscle and might, but in the unshakeable spirit of those who protect the vulnerable. "In every heart resides a lion's courage," and when summoned, this courage does not just confront, it transforms. The lion teaches us that when we stand firm, unwavering in our conviction, we do not just defy those who tower over us—we lead them.

Although, the lion leads with a dominating presence, ensuring the survival and success of its pride, it also knows that the lioness looks to their leadership and strength. In the wild, the lion's roar—a sound that can travel up to five miles—commands attention, asserts territorial dominance, and communicates power. Conversely, the lamb represents innocence, gentleness, and a calming presence, bringing a sense of peace and harmony to its surroundings.

Jesus Christ, in His earthly ministry, perfectly embodied these contrasting characteristics. As the lion, He demonstrated authoritative leadership, not shying away from challenging the status quo and confronting hypocrisy. His cleansing of the temple, driving out those who defiled it

EMBODYING DUAL MASTERY IN LEADERSHIP AND LIFE

with commerce, showcased His lion-like ferocity in defending the sanctity of worship (John 2:13-16). Yet, as the lamb, He exhibited unmatched humility and gentle submission, most poignantly symbolized by His sacrificial death on the cross (Isaiah 53:7). In these actions, Jesus illustrated that true leadership involves both the courage to stand firm and the compassion to empathize and serve.

DUAL MASTERY IN THE BOARDROOM

In business, especially in the context of boardroom dynamics, the integration of the lion and lamb characteristics fosters a leadership style that is both respected and revered. A leader, like a lion, must often take charge, make tough decisions swiftly, and guide the company through competitive terrains. This requires a commanding presence that can stir a team to action and drives them toward strategic objectives. However, the same leader, like a lamb, must also show emotional intelligence, understanding team dynamics, and nurturing a culture of trust and respect. This duality ensures that decisions are not only made with a strategic mind but also with a compassionate heart.

Starting and running a business with the dual mastery of

WHEN LAMBS TURN INTO LIONS

the lion and the lamb creates a powerful synergy. Like a lion, a business leader must pounce with precision and roar with authority, setting clear visions and making bold decisions to carve out a competitive edge. Yet, embodying the lamb, they must also foster a culture of empathy, patience, and understanding—qualities that nurture team cohesion and loyalty. Such a balance encourages innovation and dedication, essential for long-term success.

In the bustling world of entrepreneurship, the tale of Sarah and her tech startup vividly illustrates the balance of lion-like boldness and lamb-like tenderness. Sarah, a determined founder, launched her company with a lion's assertive vision—securing investments and forging ahead into the competitive tech industry. Yet, it was her lamb-like empathy that truly shaped her company's culture.

She remembered each team member's birthday, listened intently to their concerns, and fostered an environment where everyone felt valued. This blend of fierce determination and gentle leadership not only propelled her startup to achieve its early milestones but also cultivated a loyal, motivated team ready to innovate and overcome challenges together.

EMBODYING DUAL MASTERY IN LEADERSHIP AND LIFE

Sarah's story exemplifies that a leader who can charge ahead with purpose and pause with patience not only builds a successful business but also creates a thriving community within the workplace.

ILLUSTRATING LEADERSHIP IN LIFE

The confluence of these traits creates a balanced leader who can navigate the complexities of human relationships and organizational challenges with ease. This leader uses strength to protect and assertiveness to lead while employing gentleness and empathy to connect and soothe. In moments of crisis, the lion's courage and the lamb's calm coalesce, offering clear-headed decisions made with both firmness and kindness. This balance is particularly effective in negotiations, employee relations, and client management, where the ability to assert one's position without alienating others is crucial.

Beyond the boardroom, the principles of the lion and the lamb permeate all aspects of life. In family dynamics, leadership might require the lion's protective instincts, while nurturing relationships might call for the lamb's tender approach. In community involvement, the bold initiatives may need the lion's initiative, whereas resolving conflicts might benefit from the lamb's peacemaking skills.

Well, all I have written or spoken up to this point, would prove to be of no value to the reader, if practical application is avoided. To cultivate these traits, leaders can engage in reflective practices that foster self-awareness, such as meditation, journaling, or attending mentoring sessions that focus on personal growth and leadership skills. Training in conflict resolution and emotional intelligence can also enhance the ability to switch seamlessly between the lion's assertiveness and the lamb's gentleness, depending on the situation's demands.

A believer, armed with the principles of assertive leadership and compassionate humility, can effectively navigate both their spiritual journey and secular environments. By confidently demonstrating these qualities, they exemplify a kingdom perspective that integrates strength with gentleness, influencing others without compromise. This approach not only upholds their faith unapologetically but also introduces spiritual concepts subtly and effectually into non-believing settings, bridging divides and inspiring respect and curiosity.

In my final analysis and through encouraging words, I

EMBODYING DUAL MASTERY IN LEADERSHIP AND LIFE

want nothing more than to express my thoughts and observation for people that I truly desire to be successful in life—from the living room to the boardroom, male and female. The dual archetype of the lion and the lamb offers a powerful framework for understanding and developing effective leadership. By embracing both the strength of the lion and the serenity of the lamb, leaders can achieve a dynamic balance that is not only effective in managing teams and directing companies but also in leading a life that is rich with relationships and community engagement. Just as Jesus demonstrated over two millennia ago, the most impactful leaders are those who can wield power with purpose and practice compassion with courage. In the ever-evolving narrative of leadership, the synthesis of these timeless qualities continues to inspire and guide those who aspire to make a difference in the world around them and within themselves.

CHAPTER 10

A STUDY OF SILENT AUTHORITY AND GENTLE POWER

"In silence, the lion tames chaos with unwavering calm authority." —Dr. Mikel Brown

A STUDY OF SILENT AUTHORITY AND GENTLE POWER

In my personal study of material regarding lions and my observation of these wild beasts, I actually walked in the National Park in Nairobi, Kenya amongst lions. We stumbled on about seven to eight lions, lying down after a meal, and to my surprise, not one was moved or intimidated by my presence. Now, by no means am I an expert, but I am a person that has read numerous books on the life of a lion, and besides this, I watched the movie "The Lion King" many times. Laugh out loud! While observing lions in their native habitat, I have observed countless interactions that reveal the complexity of these majestic creatures. Often portrayed as the epitome of strength and ferocity, lions also exhibit a range of behaviors that align closely with qualities

WHEN LAMBS TURN INTO LIONS

traditionally associated with the lamb: gentleness, patience, and a surprising degree of restraint.

One of the most striking aspects of lion behavior is their use of silence. In the dense undergrowth of the African Savannah, a lion's silence serves as a powerful tool. Contrary to popular belief, lions do not roar frequently; they save their thunderous voices for specific moments that demand their vocal dominance. This selective use of sound is a profound lesson in leadership. Power is often most effectively wielded not by constant assertion, but by knowing when to unleash it.

During my visit in Kenya, while driving with our park's guide, I witnessed a particularly telling incident involving the pride's alpha male. This one lion was robust—his mane (hair) was a deep, sunlit gold that shimmered against the backdrop of the environment. Despite his intimidating appearance, this one lion often chose observation and presence over aggression.

The guide told me of a story of a dispute that arose among the younger males of the pride. As the conflict escalated, the alpha lion approached. He moved with deliberate slowness,

A STUDY OF SILENT AUTHORITY AND GENTLE POWER

his every step measured and calm. Instead of charging in with teeth bared, this king lion simply inserted himself between the combatants. He stood there, silent, his mere presence enough to quell the rising aggression. After a moment, he let out a single, subdued growl—not the full power of his roar, but just enough to assert his authority. The young lions, recognizing the warning, immediately ceased their skirmish and dispersed.

This king lion's behavior exemplifies the lamb-like quality of meekness, not as weakness but as controlled strength. True leaders, much like the alpha lion, understand that the loudest voice is not always the most respected or effective. There is a profound power in patience, in the quiet confidence that comes from assurance in one's strength and authority.

Moreover, the nurturing aspect of lions is another lamb-like trait. Lionesses, and sometimes males, are incredibly gentle with their cubs. I have observed lions tenderly nuzzling their young, their demeanor softening from sovereign to caretaker. This gentleness, a stark contrast to their hunting prowess, underscores a critical leadership

WHEN LAMBS TURN INTO LIONS

quality: the capacity to care.

In the wild, this balance of fierceness and kindness ensures the pride's cohesion and survival. The lions' ability to switch from one to the other seamlessly, from the ferocity required to take down a wildebeest to the gentleness needed to groom a cub, is nothing short of remarkable.

Their inquisitiveness, especially among cubs, also parallels lamb-like qualities. Lion cubs are curious about their surroundings, constantly exploring and learning. This trait is crucial for their development into effective hunters and savvy leaders of tomorrow's prides. From a zoological perspective, such curiosity is a survival mechanism—it fosters adaptability and intelligence, traits essential for any leader.

In the business world or any leadership scenario, these lessons from the lion are directly applicable. Like this alpha lion, effective leaders know when to speak and when to let their presence do the talking. This sounds like a perfect example of my mother when we would play in the house as kids. Her stare, her presence said it all. The lion leader balances strength with empathy, commands respect through calm assurance, and fosters a culture of curiosity and continuous learning.

As we seek to apply these natural principles to human endeavors, we understand that leadership is not about dominance or subjugation, but about guiding and safeguarding those in our charge. The lion, with its blend of the fierce and the gentle, serves as a powerful emblem for leaders who aspire to lead not just with force, but with heart.

In conclusion, studying lions in their natural habitat offers more than mere insights into animal behavior. It provides a blueprint for human leadership that emphasizes the balance of strength and gentleness—a dynamic duality that can transform societies and influence generations. The lion's roar may capture our attention, but it is their silent watchfulness, their patient stalking, and their nurturing care that truly encapsulate their leadership prowess. These are the qualities that make the lion not just a king of the jungle, but a leader for all seasons.

CHAPTER 11

LESSONS FOR LIFE, BUSINESS AND BEYOND

"The lion may be the king of the jungle, but even kings are called to serve." —Dr. Mikel Brown

LESSONS FOR LIFE, BUSINESS AND BEYOND

Throughout history, symbols have served as the foundation of human understanding, a means by which we comprehend greater truths. But beyond the spiritual context, these symbols carry immense practical lessons that can transform one's business, marriage, finances, and overall life. To grasp their full impact, one must delve into the characteristics of these symbols to see how they embody principles critical to success in every sphere of existence.

Life has a way of teaching us lessons through symbols, and some symbols carry weight far beyond their surface meaning. Among the most powerful are the lion and the lamb. God, in His infinite wisdom, chose these two animals to represent the fullness of Jesus Christ—both His authority and His humility, His strength and His gentleness. By studying just a fragment of their characteristics, we unlock profound truths that can transform our businesses, marriages, finances, and lives.

Imagine the lion, regal and commanding, striding across the Savanna. It is not the largest creature in its domain, yet its presence demands respect. The lion moves with purpose, conserving its energy for the right moment, never wasting effort on pursuits that do not serve its pride. This is the essence of effective leadership—knowing where to direct your focus and acting with intention.

In business, this approach can be life-changing. How often do we find ourselves overwhelmed, chasing every opportunity, yet achieving little? The lion teaches us that success requires discipline and a clear vision. When we focus on what truly matters, we begin to lead with authority, earning respect not because of our size or resources, but because of the clarity and confidence with which we move.

In the marketplace, authority doesn't necessarily stem

from size or initial resources, but from confidence and clarity of vision. The lion moves with purpose, understanding that it doesn't need to chase every opportunity, but focuses on what will sustain and grow its pride. Similarly, businesses and individuals flourish when they operate with intentionality. Entrepreneurs often fail not because of a lack of potential, but because they chase every opportunity rather than refining their focus. By adopting the lion's disciplined approach, leaders can direct their energies toward ventures that yield the highest impact.

Now, picture the lion in the context of marriage. Its strength is not in dominance but in protection and provision. The lion is fiercely loyal to its pride, standing guard against threats and ensuring the safety of those it loves. In a marriage, this kind of strength is indispensable. It's about being a partner who offers security—not just financially, but emotionally and spiritually. Strong marriages are built on this kind of unwavering commitment, where each partner feels safe and valued.

But then, there is the lamb—a creature that could not be

more different from the lion. Where the lion is bold and commanding, the lamb is gentle and unassuming. You can't imagine how many times I've been told that I am so unassuming. I personally like it that way because I'd rather be known for the content of my character than by disclosing my personal assets.

The strength of the lamb lies in its humility, its willingness to be vulnerable. At first glance, the lamb might seem weak, but it is precisely this vulnerability that gives it such profound power. The lamb teaches us that true greatness often comes from humility.

Consider how this plays out in leadership. Leaders who embody the humility of the lamb inspire trust and loyalty. They listen more than they speak, serve rather than demand, and prioritize the well-being of their team over their own ego. This is the kind of leadership that transforms organizations—not through fear or control, but through service and compassion. When people feel valued and heard, they flourish, and so does the organization.

Matthew 20:25 But Jesus called them

together and said, "You know that the rulers in this world lord it over their people, and officials flaunt their authority over those under them. 26 But among you it will be different. Whoever wants to be a leader among you must be your servant, 27 and whoever wants to be first among you must become your slave. 28 For even the Son of Man came not to be served but to serve others and to give his life as a ransom for many." (NLT)

In relationships, the lamb's lesson of sacrifice is equally profound. Love, at its core, is about putting someone else's needs above your own. This does not mean losing yourself or becoming a doormat; it means understanding that sometimes, the greatest gift you can give is your willingness to step back and prioritize the union over individual desires. Sacrifice, when given freely and out of love, becomes a source of strength, not weakness.

Even in finances, the lamb and the lion provide a surprising blueprint. Managing money requires the boldness of the lion—taking risks, seizing opportunities, and moving with confidence. But it also demands the caution and integrity of the lamb—avoiding shortcuts, staying ethical, and being wise with resources. The balance between courage and prudence is what leads to true financial stability and growth.

The deeper truth, though, lies in the fact that the lion and the lamb are not opposing forces; they are complementary. Jesus Christ embodies both, showing us that strength and humility, authority and gentleness, are not contradictions. They are two sides of the same coin. To live fully, we must learn to embrace both.

In your business, you might need the lion's boldness to make tough decisions, but the lamb's humility will guide you to lead with compassion. In your marriage, you might draw on the lion's strength to protect and provide, but the lamb's gentleness will nurture intimacy and trust. In your finances, the lion's courage will help you take calculated risks, while the lamb's discipline will ensure you avoid greed and maintain integrity.

LESSONS FOR LIFE, BUSINESS AND BEYOND

God's choice of the lion and the lamb to represent Jesus is a divine message for humanity. The lion shows us how to lead, protect, and act with courage. The lamb reminds us to serve, sacrifice, and walk in humility. Together, they form a model for living a life of purpose, balance, and impact.

When you adopt the lion's authority and the lamb's humility, you begin to live with a new kind of power—one that is not loud or aggressive, but steady and enduring. This balance allows you to face challenges with courage and wisdom, lead with strength and compassion, and build relationships rooted in trust and sacrifice.

The journey of embracing both the lion and the lamb is transformative. It requires you to look beyond the surface, to delve into your own life and ask: Where do I need more courage? Where do I need more humility? As you answer these questions, you will find that the principles embodied by the lion and the lamb begin to permeate every aspect of your life, guiding you toward a deeper understanding of yourself and your purpose.

Ultimately, the lion and the lamb show us that true

success—whether in business, marriage, finances, or life—is not about choosing one path over the other. It's about embracing the fullness of both. When you do, you align yourself with God's design, positioning yourself for a life of abundance, impact, and eternal significance.

This is the legacy of the lion and the lamb—a legacy that invites us to live with strength, lead with humility, and transform our world with the balance of both. Now, let's continue to explore the richness of the lion and the lamb, weaving it into an immersive narrative of transformation, motivation, and inspiration.

As you reflect on the lion and the lamb, imagine yourself standing on the edge of a vast Savanna at dusk. The horizon is alive with golden hues, and in the distance, you hear the mighty roar of a lion. It is a call that commands attention, a reminder that you are in the presence of greatness. Yet, not far from where you stand, a gentle lamb grazes, peaceful and unafraid. It is a scene of profound contrast and balance, one that whispers to your soul about the tension and harmony that must exist within you if you are to thrive.

LESSONS FOR LIFE, BUSINESS AND BEYOND

This is not just a lesson—it is an invitation. An invitation to rise above mediocrity, to step into your God-given purpose with the boldness of a lion while remaining anchored in the humility of a lamb. The question is, are you ready to embrace the power of these truths? Because doing so will require courage. It will demand introspection and action, faith and resolve. But make no mistake, it will also lead to transformation beyond your imagination.

> "The lion may be the king of the jungle, but even kings are called to serve." —Dr. Mikel Brown

Consider for a moment the lion's roar. It is not merely noise; it is a declaration of dominion. When the lion roars, it stakes its claim, reminding everything within earshot that it rules this territory. Is that not what life demands of us? To rise each day and declare dominion—not over others, but over ourselves, our fears, our doubts, and our circumstances?

Life is not for the timid, and neither is success. The marketplace will not hand you a crown, nor will marriage flourish without intentional effort. Finances do not grow on their own, and your purpose will not fulfill itself while you sit idly by. You must roar. You must claim your space, set your boundaries, and let the world know that you are here to make an impact.

Here is where the lamb enters the scene. A lion that roars without reason becomes a tyrant, feared but not loved. And love, as the lamb teaches us, is the ultimate currency. The lamb whispers what the lion cannot: that power is not in the roar alone but in the tenderness that follows it. Strength and authority without love are empty; love without strength is powerless. Together, they are unstoppable.

> "Sacrifice is the currency of greatness."
> —Dr. Mikel Brown

Think about that for a moment. The lamb's life is a life of sacrifice. It gives itself freely, not out of weakness, but out of a profound understanding of purpose. When Jesus walked the earth, He did so as the Lamb of God, willingly laying down His life for others. In doing so, He showed us that the greatest victories are not won by force but by surrender.

This truth applies to every area of life. In business, you may be called to sacrifice short-term comfort for long-term success. In marriage, you might need to set aside your pride to build a relationship that lasts. In your finances, you may have to sacrifice immediate gratification to create a legacy of wealth and stability. Sacrifice is not about loss; it's about exchange. It is trading what is temporary for what is eternal, what is fleeting for what is foundational.

> "Be bold enough to roar, but wise enough to graze." —Dr. Mikel Brown

The lion and the lamb teach us that life is not a single pursuit but a dance between power and peace, action and stillness, ambition and humility. As you navigate your journey, you will face moments when you must roar, standing firm and making your presence known. You will also encounter seasons when grazing, observing, and moving with quiet wisdom is the only way forward.

Take the example of a successful entrepreneur. At the start, they may need the lion's courage to launch their business, facing risks and critics head-on. But as the business grows, the lamb's qualities—gentleness, patience, and the ability to nurture relationships—become the foundation of sustained success. Roaring at every stage would alienate partners and employees; grazing too long would result in missed opportunities. The balance of both is what propels greatness.

> "Every lion was once a cub, every lamb was once unsteady on its feet." — Dr. Mikel Brown

You may feel unqualified or ill-prepared to embody these qualities. That's natural. Nobody is born knowing how to lead with authority or how to love sacrificially. These are learned behaviors, shaped by time, experience, and divine guidance. The lion's roar is developed through practice; the lamb's humility is cultivated through surrender.

Think back to a time when you were at your lowest, uncertain of how to move forward. That moment was your training ground. It was teaching you to roar in the face of adversity and to trust in the stillness of surrender. Every setback, every heartache, every failure has been refining you, preparing you for this moment—the moment when you step into your destiny as both lion and lamb.

> "The weight of the crown is lightened by the humility of the heart." —Dr. Mikel Brown

When you truly embrace the lion and the lamb, you begin to understand that leadership—whether in your business, your family, or your community—is not about the crown you wear but the people you serve. The lion protects its pride, not for personal gain, but because its strength is meant for others. The lamb sacrifices itself, not out of obligation, but because its love compels it to give.

Imagine what your life would look like if you lived this way. If you approached your career with the lion's boldness and the lamb's humility. If you led your family with strength and compassion. If you managed your finances with courage and discipline. The ripple effect would be immeasurable. You would inspire others to do the same, creating a legacy that outlasts you.

> "Roar when it's time to roar, kneel when it's time to kneel." —Dr. Mikel Brown

Timing is everything. There is a time to stand tall and fight, to claim your place and assert your authority. But there is also a time to kneel, to humble yourself and acknowledge that true strength comes from surrender. The lion teaches you to stand firm; the lamb reminds you to bow low. Together, they guide you through life's seasons with wisdom and grace. Sometimes, you have to come back to fight another day.

Picture yourself five years from now, living as both lion and lamb. Your business is thriving because you have led with courage and integrity. Your marriage is stronger because you have loved sacrificially and fought for unity. Your finances are secure because you have balanced boldness with wisdom. Most importantly, your soul is at peace because you have walked in alignment with God's design.

This is the power of the lion and the lamb. It is not just a metaphor; it is a lifestyle. A call to rise higher, love deeper, and lead better. To live with the fortitude of a lion and the grace of a lamb is to live a life that is not only successful but significant.

So, what will you do with this revelation? Will you step

into your destiny, roaring when it's time to roar and kneeling when it's time to kneel? Will you embrace the tension and harmony of the lion and the lamb, allowing them to transform every area of your life? The choice is yours. But remember this: the world needs more leaders who roar with courage and serve with humility. It needs more people like you, willing to live as both lion and lamb.

The lion roars. The lamb grazes. And together, they change the world.

CHAPTER 12

MY PERSONAL TRANSFORMATION FROM LAMB TO LION

"The lamb's weakness forges the ultimate lion's strength." —Dr. Mikel Brown

MY PERSONAL TRANSFORMATION FROM LAMB TO LION

There was a time in my life when I felt like I had all the answers, but in reality, I was lost. Drugs, insecurity, and a bad attitude defined me. I lived my life with the sole purpose of manipulating and using people to get what I wanted, without regard for how it affected them. My life was spiraling out of control, and the truth is, I didn't care—until I reached a point where everything I relied on crumbled before my eyes.

I grew up with the false notion that strength was measured by how much I could take from others, by how much I could assert my will, even if it meant stepping on the backs of those around me. Trust was a foreign concept, and faith was something I scoffed at. I was my own god, or so I thought. But deep down, behind the bravado and attitude, was a boy crying out for help, lost in the darkness of my own choices.

Drugs became my escape, a means to drown the insecurities that constantly gnawed at my soul. Insecurity about my worth, my abilities, and my purpose in life. I thought if I could control my environment—manipulate people and circumstances—I could gain the power and satisfaction I was seeking. But that power was fleeting, and satisfaction never came. The more I pursued it, the emptier I became. The cycle was vicious, and the deeper I sank into it, the more hopeless I felt.

I vividly remember the day everything came crashing down. I was at the lowest point of my life, alone in a dark room, numb from the drugs, angry at the world, and disgusted with myself. I had alienated the people closest to me, and there was no more ground to stand on. I was at rock bottom. It was in that moment, when I had nothing left, that something stirred inside me. It was small, a whisper—almost unnoticeable—but it was there. A voice

MY PERSONAL TRANSFORMATION FROM LAMB TO LION

telling me that this wasn't the end, that my life had a purpose beyond the chaos I had created.

It took a while for that whisper to grow louder, but eventually, it became something I could no longer ignore. I remember the first time I heard about Jesus Christ. I wasn't interested at first. I had always viewed faith as a crutch for the weak, for people who couldn't handle life's challenges. But the more I resisted, the more I felt drawn to this message of grace, redemption, and purpose. I was curious, but more than that, I was desperate.

One day, I found myself in a church, not knowing what to expect. I sat in the back, arms crossed, determined to keep my distance. But the words of the preacher broke through every wall I had built around my heart. He spoke about Jesus as the Lamb of God—humble, selfless, willing to lay down His life for others. But he also spoke about Jesus as the Lion of Judah—a powerful, victorious King who conquers sin, death, and everything that oppresses us. That combination of humility and power hit me like a ton of bricks.

I had been living like a predator, thinking that strength was found in how much I could dominate, manipulate, or destroy. But Jesus demonstrated a different kind of strength—a strength found in submission to the will of God, in sacrifice, and in love. The lion inside of me wasn't meant to devour; it was meant to defend, to protect, to uplift others. It was at that moment I realized the lion and the lamb could coexist. That was the beginning of my transformation.

As I gave my life to Christ, I started to learn the principles that would reshape everything I thought I knew about life, business, and faith. The first thing the Holy Spirit taught me was the power of surrender. I had spent my entire life trying to control everything, but true strength, I learned, came from submitting to God's will. This wasn't weakness; it was the greatest form of power, because in my surrender, God's power began to flow through me.

Faith became my new foundation. The Bible became my guidebook for life, and I started to see that the same power that raised Christ from the dead was available to me as a believer. It wasn't about speaking empty words or positive thinking; it was about speaking God's Word with faith, knowing that His promises are true and powerful. In business, I began to apply these principles. Instead of

MY PERSONAL TRANSFORMATION FROM LAMB TO LION

manipulating and taking advantage of others, I learned the value of integrity, honor, and trust. As I walked in faith, God blessed my efforts in ways I couldn't have imagined.

Money, which had once been an idol in my life, was no longer the measure of my success. Instead, I learned that true prosperity comes from aligning with God's purposes and trusting Him as my source. The more I gave, the more I received—not just in material wealth, but in peace, joy, and relationships. The principles of generosity, stewardship, and faith in God's provision transformed my approach to finances, and I saw Him move in miraculous ways.

But perhaps the greatest lesson I learned was about confidence. My old confidence was based on insecurity, on trying to prove myself to the world. But now, my confidence was rooted in my identity as a child of God. I no longer felt the need to strike back at every challenge or attack. I no longer had to defend myself with my fists or my words. I had the confidence to stand firm, knowing that the battle belonged to the Lord. No matter the size of the challenge, I could face it with peace, because I knew who was fighting for me.

WHEN LAMBS TURN INTO LIONS

The more I walked with Jesus, the more I realized that the lion had been inside me all along, but I had been misusing its power. I was trying to be the king of my own life, but in Christ, I found my true identity as both lion and lamb. I learned to walk with humility, but also with authority. I learned that faith wasn't just about believing in God, but about living in the fullness of who He created me to be. The lion that was in the Lamb is in all of us who believe in Christ. It's not about dominating others; it's about walking in the power and purpose that God has called us to.

My life is a testimony of how Jesus transforms the broken, the lost, and the misguided into warriors for His kingdom. Through His Spirit, I have learned to live with purpose, integrity, and faith. I've learned to trust in God's provision, to speak His Word with authority, and to face every challenge with the confidence that comes from knowing who I am in Him. Just as the lion was in the Lamb, that same power is within every believer, waiting to be unleashed.

We are called to live as both—humble and powerful, surrendered to God and walking in His authority. This is the life of transformation. This is the power of faith in Jesus

MY PERSONAL TRANSFORMATION FROM LAMB TO LION

Christ. And, the amazing thing for me was that no one forced or manipulated me to make my decision to accept Jesus as my Lord—I did it on my own. Somehow, I knew for the first time in my life, it was the right thing to do.

Jesus offers love, peace, and purpose like no one else. He knows you fully and desires a personal relationship with you. No matter where you've been or what you've done, His arms are open. By accepting Jesus as your Savior, you receive forgiveness, hope, and a new life. Simply invite Him into your heart, talk to Him, and trust in His love. He will guide you every step of the way. I'm a living witness!

PLATINUM PRINCIPLES

"Learn to command respect like a lion, offer solace like a lamb, but master both for success."

"The Lamb's grace transforms into the Lion's unstoppable courage."

"Humility roots you; boldness empowers you to reign as a lion."

"Humility grounds us; boldness leads us in life's fiercest battles."

"In unity, lambs rise as an impenetrable force of purpose."

"Through challenges, resilience is built; through faith, the lion emerges."

"Bold leadership requires precise action, strategic wisdom, and fearless faith."

"It is this fluidity, this seamless transition from lion to lamb and back, that transforms people and communities."

"In every heart resides a lion's courage," and when summoned, this courage does not just confront, it transforms."

"In silence, the lion tames chaos with unwavering calm authority."

"The lamb's weakness forges the ultimate lion's strength."

"The lion may be the king of the jungle, but even kings are called to serve."

ABOUT THE AUTHOR

Any successful business owner knows that starting from the bottom has as much to do with success as having a vision, and Dr. Mikel Brown knows this all too well. Dr. Brown says, "Everyone starts from the bottom, and those that start from the top, are ditch diggers."

Dr. Mikel Brown has been in the financial industry for more than forty years and has established businesses from restaurants to staffing companies. He has also conducted financial and business seminars with Mark Victor Hansen the co-author of the Chicken Soup for the Soul series, Dr. Mike Murdock, as well as with other national seminar speakers. Dr. Brown is an ordained minister of over 40 years and is the senior pastor of Christian Joy Center and overseer of ECCM churches. He is the author of over 13 books to include Building Wealth from the Ground Up, Unexpected Treasures, and Turn On Your Life, Dream Big, Start Small, just to name a few.

UNLEASH THE POWER TO
MAKE LIFE WORK FOR YOU

TURN ON YOUR LIFE

Turn On Your Life is a realistic, down-to-earth approach on how to turn your mistakes into miracles, your breakdowns into breakthroughs and your disappointments into divine appointments with destiny. There is nothing more exhilarating than knowing that where you presently are, is part of the process to getting to where you always wanted to be.

Here are seven chapters that will peak your interest:

- Seven Ordinary Rules For Extraordinary Results
- Disarming Pressure And Stress
- Contract And Build The Life And Business Of Your Dreams
- Don't Wait For The Chance Of A Lifetime
- Greatness Is A Decision Away
- Life's Purpose Is Discovered While Helping Others Find Theirs
- Wisdom For A Better Life

SCAN TO GET YOUR COPY
TODAY!

ISBN: 978-1-930388-21-5 (Paperback) Retail: $14.95
ISBN: 978-1-930388-22-2 (Hardback) Retail: $18.95

A Bold New Release From
Dr. Mikel A. Brown

DREAM BIG
START SMALL

AWAKEN THE ENTREPRENEUR WITHIN

Sets itself apart from other business self-help books by integrating the essential role of faith and spirituality in achieving success. This distinctive guide not only offers a beginner-friendly approach to starting a business but also highlights the importance of trusting in God's plan and recognizing His divine hand in one's journey.

Learn how to find your passion, build a brand around it, and get paid doing what makes you happy!

SCAN TO GET YOUR COPY
TODAY!

Get Connected and Stay Connected!
Connect, Subscribe, and Follow Dr. Mikel Brown

@drmikelbrown_ / Facebook: Dr. Mikel Brown / @drmikelbrown / @BishopMikelBrown

www.MikelBrown.com

www.ingramcontent.com/pod-product-compliance
Lightning Source LLC
Chambersburg PA
CBHW020754230426
43673CB00022B/437/J